STRATEGIC SALES PLAN
WHY SALES FAIL AND HOW WINS ARE WON

STRATEGIC SALES PLAN
WHY SALES FAIL AND HOW WINS ARE WON

Copyright: © 2018, Robert P. DeGroot, MEd, DCH

All Rights Reserved. No part of this work may be reproduced or stored by any means without the written approval of the author (except brief excerpts used in published reviews).

Customized Editions: For information about customized editions and corporate sales, please contact Sales Training International 1-281-367-5599 Info@SalesHelp.com

Published by: Sales Training International
5781 Cape Harbour Drive STE 607
Cape Coral, Florida 33914
1-281-367-5599
www.SalesHelp.com

ISBN: 978-0-9864058-7-7 (Paperback)
ISBN: 978-0-9864058-6-0 (e-book: .ePub)

Edition 4 Date: 070218

Table of Contents

Introduction
Milestones to Sales Success
Instructions for Using this Book

Profile and Qualify the Sales Prospect 1
1. Compare the prospect with the profile of your most desirable customers. 1
2. Identify decision-makers. 2
3. Identify the initial people to contact. 4
4. Select and sequence methods of contact. 5
5. Set call objectives. 7
6. Make contact. 8
7. Establish trust and rapport. 10
8. Qualify the prospect for the current sales opportunity. 12

Research the Prospect's Needs 14
9. Research prospect's products, services, and company. 14
10. Research the prospect's critical processes. 16
11. Research prospect's business plan. 18
12. Identify the potential for your other products and services. 19

Conduct the Competitor Analyses 21
13. Identify your external and internal competitors. 21
14. Conduct the competitor analyses. 22
15. Update your list of Unique Selling Points. 23
16. Identify potential objections. 25

Establish the Value of What You Sell 28

17. Prevent, preempt, and respond to potential objections. 28
18. Focus the topics of conversation on your Unique Selling Points (USPs). 29
19. Identify the signs caused by your USPs' missing Advantages and Benefits. 31
20. Confirm the problems caused by the missing USPs. 33
21. Quantify their costs of not having your USPs to establish the value of the solution. 35
22. Set your USPs as specifications that must be met to solve the problems. 38
23. Competitor Proof with Benefits Questions. 40
24. Complete the interviews with key decision makers. 42
25. Validate any cost-benefit data that used industry standards. 43

Complete the Logistics Steps 44

26. Advise and get agreement on the next steps to advance the sale. 44
27. Outline feedback loops, milestones, measurements, and follow-up process. 46
28. Develop product/service delivery phase-in plans. 48
29. Determine product/service availability. 49
30. Complete required pre-purchase approvals. 50
31. Exchange any additional data, specifications, or financial information. 52
32. Identify and prepare your Recommenders to be your Champions. 53

Propose, Present, and Negotiate 54

33. Prepare and submit the Customer Value Proposition (CVP) 54
34. Conduct sales presentation using the CVP format. 56
35. Prospect affirms your ability to meet the criteria. 58
36. Conclude final negotiations. 59
37. Final budget approval received. 61
38. Contract signed, or letter of engagement received. 62
39. Customer notifies current supplier(s). 63

Deliver Your Products & Services 65

40. Identify and arrange to meet the critical support people. ...65
41. Identify specific End Users involved in the project. 67
42. Conduct quality checks of the product and service delivery. 68

Manage Your Account 70

43. Implement sales activities to competitor proof and grow the account. 70
44. Recognize the signs your account may be in trouble before it's too late. 73

Resources Specific to the Strategic Sales Plan 75
Glossary of Terms 76
Differentiating Factors 95
Strategic Sales Plan 97
About the Author 100
Other books by Robert DeGroot 101

Introduction

The Strategic Sales Plan is designed to help you identify the steps in your sales process that must be done to win business to business sales.

Beginning in 1988 and up to the present time, we analyzed thousands of sales, across industries, to discover why sales failed and how they were won.

This research led to a comprehensive diagnostic sales process consisting of 44 essential steps in the consultative value selling process used by Sales Professionals who sell solutions to meet their customers' functional, business, and human needs.

The objective is to find your patterns of steps, which when missed, cause sales to fail and to find the pattern of steps that when done, cause sales to be won.

Get started by validating each step for what you sell and then review your sales to find your patterns for both losses and wins.

At the end of this process, you'll have a validated checklist of sales process steps for what you sell that you can use to guide you to "win more sales." Now that's a great sales tool.

Dr. Robert DeGroot

Milestones to Sales Success

The sales process steps are assigned to milestones.

The percentages represent the probability that the sale will be won when that milestone is achieved.

The percentages and milestones below are based on the logic of this Strategic Sales Plan. Once you complete your validation of the steps, you can then establish what's within each milestone for what you sell.

The goal is to have some mutually agreed upon percentages for each milestone based on the steps completed in your sales process. Now when you say you've got a 50% chance of winning the sale, you will know that steps 1-25 are complete.

Percent / Milestone / Steps Completed

- 10%   Profile and Qualify the Sales Prospect (Steps 1-8)
- 20%   Research the Prospect's Needs (Steps 9-12)
- 30%   Conduct the Competitor Analysis (Steps 13-16)
- 50%   Establish the Value of What You Sell (Steps 17-25)
- 70%   Complete the Logistics Steps (Steps 26-32)
- 80%   Propose, Present, and Negotiate (Steps 33-39)
- 90%   Deliver Your Products & Services (Steps 40-42)
- 100% Manage Your Account (Steps 43-44)

Instructions for Using this Book

1. **Validate** the steps you need to do for what you sell by identifying the consequences of not doing each of them. Cross off, add, or modify steps.

2. **Analyze** a dozen losses, and a dozen wins to find the patterns of steps missed that caused your sales to fail and the patterns of steps that were done that caused your sales to be won.

3. **Learn the skills** you need so you can readily complete steps that are difficult for you.

Profile and Qualify the Sales Prospect

1. **Compare the prospect with the profile of your most desirable customers.**

The purpose of this step is to identify characteristics of your most desirable customers so that you have a profile to use to locate and qualify other similar companies (prospects).

Characteristics to consider include:

- Market, market segment, and industry group.
- Size: How much do they use? Categorize A, B, C based on account potential (add AAA, AA, A+ or D size if needed).
- Values: How closely do their core corporate values match yours and your company's? The closer the match, the easier the sale.
- Territory: Where are your customers located?
- Other characteristics for what you sell?

Action items to complete this step:

- Create a list of characteristics your most desirable customers have in common:
- Compare these characteristics with your most desirable customers to qualify them or to identify what it will take to qualify them.
- Identify resources to find similar prospects that could potentially meet the profile.

Consequences:

What are the consequences if this step is not done?

STRATEGIC SALES PLAN

2. Identify decision-makers.

Within each sale, there are different types of decisions to make. One person could make several of these decisions, or several people may make just one.

The role they play in the organization determines the types of decisions they make, and the types of Benefits your Unique Selling Points (USPs) provide that are important to them.

Make sure you know who the decision makers are in each sales opportunity.

Decision Maker Roles:

1. **Final Authority:** Interested in Return on Investment (ROI), Rate of Return (ROR), and confidence in getting the results. *How much, how soon, how sure?*
2. **Specifier**: Interested in performance specifications and cost justification. *How do I know it will do what you say it will? How can I justify the cost?*
3. **Negotiator:** Interested in "top-line" price, terms and conditions, and warranties. Price to Feature Ratio. *How can I be sure I'm getting the best deal?*
4. **Consumer or End User:** Focus is on capabilities and user-friendliness. *How easy is it to use?*
5. **Coach:** Concerned about capability and credibility and the level of trust and rapport they have with you. Once you gain a certain level of trust, the person will guide you through the process. Add the coaching role to the other decision makers. *Why should I trust you?*
6. **Recommender:** Interested in capabilities and credibility. *What capabilities and credibility do you have that'll help the customer and make me look good?*

Bias:
- Champion (Mentor)
- Favorable (Sponsor)

Profile and Qualify the Sales Prospect

- Neutral
- Unfavorable
- Blocker

Action items to complete this step:

- Identify each of the decision makers in your sale by the type of decisions they make.
- Know the general type of benefits each decision maker is most interested in discussing.
- Determine the specific benefits you can offer from your Unique Selling Points that appeal to each of the decision-makers.
- Uncover and manage "Bias."

Consequences:

What are the consequences if this step is not done?

STRATEGIC SALES PLAN

3. Identify the initial people to contact.

Who do you normally contact first? And next? And next?

What is the most advantageous sequence to contact people within a specific company?

Action items to complete this step:

- Determine the decision-maker to contact first based on:
    - Strength of Unique Selling Points' Benefits
    - Ability to make contact
    - Ability to develop into a coach
- Establish a sequence in which you would prefer to make contact with each of the different decision-makers.
    - ____ Final Authority
    - ____ Specifier
    - ____ Negotiator
    - ____ End User
    - ____ Coach
    - ____ Recommender

Consequences:

What are the consequences if this step is not done?

Profile and Qualify the Sales Prospect

4. Select and sequence methods of contact.

Don't limit your contact methods to just one or two. Be flexible and select the methods most appropriate for the decision-makers.

Use the following list of prospecting contact methods (different from marketing methods such as ads, sponsoring, broadcast, etc.) to help determine the type, sequence, and frequency necessary for this sales opportunity.

- Phone (cold or warm calls)
- Voicemail commercials
- Mail
    - Brochures
    - Interest mail (based on business, position, profession)
    - Postcards
    - Flyers
    - 1st class letters
- E-mail
    - Direct contact
    - Press Releases
    - Passive email series
    - Interest email series
    - Keep in touch series
- In-person
    - Cold call
    - Networking (professional, trade, business events, galas, charity events, etc.)
- Networking online, i.e., LinkedIn
- Referral contact
- Prospect trade show exhibitors

Action items to complete this step:

- Select the preferred methods of contact.

STRATEGIC SALES PLAN

- Create a sequence of methods so that the probability of contact increases.
- Determine an effective frequency of contact attempts.
- Set a strategy to contact multiple decision makers in the same organization using multiple methods of contact to prevent getting blocked by a single decision maker.

Consequences:

What are the consequences if this step is not done?

Profile and Qualify the Sales Prospect

5. Set call objectives.

The steps you validate for this Strategic Sales Plan become the foundation for your master list of "call-objectives."

Continue to identify steps until there isn't an undiscovered step left for your own master plan. Know that as you complete each step, you are advancing the sale toward closure. You want to know all the steps you must do to win your sales.

Notice the structure of this Strategic Sales Plan. First, you have the Step stated as an objective, and then you have action items.

To complete this step with a real prospect, you would add the time-limits to stay within the sales cycle, a way to know you've done them (checklist), and the source for the resources you need (that are not readily available).

Action items to complete this step:

- Write call objectives as goals with time-limited measurable targets.
- Identify and plan action items that must be carried out to accomplish the objective.
- Tie the action items into a time management process to ensure their completion in a timely manner.
- Identify and acquire the resources necessary to carry out the objectives.

Consequences:

What are the consequences if this step is not done?

Strategic Sales Plan

6. Make contact.

You'll initially need to use standard differentiators or Unique Selling Points (USPs) specific to your products, services, company, and self.

You find these by conducting several competitor analyses and selecting those that continue to show up again and again against different competitors.

Build your USPs into your opening remarks elevator speech (phone, email, etc.) to prevent common initial contact objections such as, "not interested," "already have someone," and "just send me your literature."

Final preparation for this step is to get mentally prepared for the contact. Just as athletes can hurt themselves physically if they don't warm up before engaging in strenuous activity, you can also hurt yourself psychologically if you don't warm up mentally.

You've read enough emails where you could tell something was off about the writer; perhaps they were tired, bored, or angry. Your mental attitude will often show up during your interactions – especially in person.

Action items to complete this step:

- Select three standard Unique Selling Points for the decision maker you're contacting.
- Review objection prevent, preempt, and respond strategies for common initial contact objections that you've used successfully in the past.
- Review initial contact script outline or bullet points and critical concepts to prevent common initial contact objections.
- Warm-up mentally by reading inspirational sayings, using positive self-talk, reviewing how your company

Profile and Qualify the Sales Prospect

helps its customers meet their needs. Feel good about the Unique Selling Points you can bring to the prospective customer.

Consequences:

What are the consequences if this step is not done?

7. Establish trust and rapport.

Nothing happens in sales without some level of trust and rapport. Making contact with prospects requires the ability to establish trust and rapport quickly. Customers often decide to buy from you first, before they decide what they're going to buy.

Trust means to believe without proof.
Rapport means to be in harmony.

The process of building trust and rapport begins with the initial contact. For example, "pacing and leading" takes only seconds and can create a deep level of personal rapport.

Common methods to establish personal trust and rapport:

- Pacing and leading
- Common Ground
- Credentials
- Psychological Truth (Active Listening Skills)
- Research Questions (on target)
- Benefits Questions (Creating Attitudes)
- Referrals

Capability means you can do what you say you can do.
Credibility means believability. You do what you say you will do.

Your company's product literature can establish initial perceptions of capability and credibility just by its look, touch, and feel.

Common methods to establish corporate capability and credibility:

- Well-designed website
- Corporate capability and credibility brochures

Profile and Qualify the Sales Prospect

- Testimonials and References
- Partial (relevant) client list
- Prospect's strategic initiatives (link your USPs to them)

Action items to complete this step:

- Select, use, and monitor effectiveness of specific methods to establish personal trust and rapport for each decision maker.
- Select, use, and monitor effectiveness of specific methods to promote corporate capability and credibility for each decision maker.

Consequences:

What are the consequences if this step is not done?

8. Qualify the prospect for the current sales opportunity.

Compare your list of descriptive characteristics your most desirable customers have in common with this prospect or current customer project.

Any discrepancies you uncover can help you determine if you or the prospect have the capabilities needed to make this opportunity viable.

Action Items to complete this step:

- Determine the extent to which this prospect or project meets the profile of your most desirable customers and projects.
- Determine what it would take to fix any disqualifying discrepancies.
- Develop a master list of internal decision-makers and influences.
- Develop a master list of external decision-makers and influences (bankers, governments, interest groups, etc.).
- Create an organizational chart to help discern if anyone was missed that might be crucial to this project.
- Identify any political influence amongst the various decision-makers and their direct reports.
- Determine if you are going to be able to interview or cover each of them within the sales cycle. Covering a decision maker means that you developed a champion who can sell to the person you cannot reach.

GO / NO GO

"**GO / NO GO**" simply means that if this step is not complete, the sale cannot or should not move forward. For this step, it comes down acknowledging that if the prospect is not qualified, there is no reason to continue to pursue this opportunity.

Profile and Qualify the Sales Prospect

You can choose which steps to make "GO / NO GO" so they are relevant to what you sell.

Consequences:

What are the consequences if this step is not done?

Research the Prospect's Needs

9. Research prospect's products, services, and company.

With this step, you're primarily looking for ways your Unique Selling Points can competitively advantage the prospective customer in their marketplace.

This could include finding ways in which what you sell, could make their products, services, and company better in some way that has value to them or their customers.

You earn customer loyalty because your Unique Selling Points are having a profound positive effect on the customer's success. This effect could be in a small clearly defined area or on the business as a whole.

Either way, what your Unique Selling Points provide gives them highly desirable benefits used internally or an effective advantage externally over their competitors.

Action Items to complete this step:

- Look at your prospect's customers and how they use their products and services to find areas where what you sell could make that better.
- Determine the cost to switch to what you sell versus the cost to stay with the current way of doing things. Include the financial (profits and costs), subjective (hassle), and emotional (frustration) costs of not having your Unique Selling Points.
- Identify how you can competitively advantage this prospect in their marketplace through the use of what you sell

Research the Prospect's Needs

- Identify how your Unique Selling Points can have a profound effect on the customer's success.

Consequences:

What are the consequences if this step is not done?

10. Research the prospect's critical processes.

How does the prospect make money and how can you impact their ability to make money?

How are they currently getting their needs met and how can you improve that process?

Types of needs:

- **Functional Needs:** These are met by what your product or service does. For example, a car fills the Functional Need for transportation. Focus on the Functional needs met by your Unique Selling Points.
- **Business Needs:**
    o Increase ability to generate profitable revenue
    o Lower costs of operation
    o Strengthen their image
    o Reduce their vulnerability
- **Human Needs:**
    o Money needs
    o Safety needs
    o Esteem needs
    o Pleasure needs

Since you may not have yet identified your competitors, nor conducted specific competitor analysis, use your standard Unique Selling Points (USPs) common in previous sales activities with similar opportunities, to make your initial determinations.

Action items to complete this step:

- How is the prospect currently getting their Functional Needs met?
- Who is the current supplier?
- Map the steps the prospect goes through to get the targeted benefits.

Research the Prospect's Needs

- Focus on those steps where you can have a positive impact on their results.
- What are the USPs you can apply to enhance their ability to get their Functional (what the USP does), Business, and Human Needs met?
- What other needs can your USPs meet that would significantly benefit the customer? These are often needs the prospect doesn't know they have, or if they know they have them, they didn't know there is a solution available to fill them.
- Identify other processes you could potentially impact.

Consequences:

What are the consequences if this step is not done?

STRATEGIC SALES PLAN

11. Research prospect's business plan.

Where can you fit into your prospect's business plans?

What areas should you look for and monitor that could impact your ability to sell to this prospect?

For example:

- **Timing:** What is the "buying cycle" for what you sell? What is the prospect's current target date for purchase? Can you complete your sales cycle in time?
- **Budget:** Has a budget been established or will you have to create one by establishing the value of what you sell?
- **Stability:** Is this prospect growing, shrinking, or holding steady? Are they profitable? Will you be extending credit?
- **Organizational Change:** Are there any organizational changes that will impact your ability to do business with this prospect?
- **Strategic Initiatives:** What major projects will the prospect take on that you can support with your Unique Selling Points and other capabilities?

Action items to complete this step:

- Develop a list of areas to monitor that can impact your ability to sell to this prospect (and "industry group").
- Identify any strategic initiatives you can support with your Unique Selling Points.
- Know the questions to ask and who to ask to acquire the necessary information about the business plan.

Consequences:

What are the consequences if this step is not done?

12. Identify the potential for your other products and services.

Often companies will have several related product and service lines they can sell to the same buyers. It makes sense to build your sales sequence starting with the most likely to be successful product or service, and then determine logically and strategically what should come next.

Cross-selling, upselling, and add-on selling, are all a part of this strategy. On occasion, the additional products and services can be brought into the current sales opportunity to make the purchase more productive and satisfying to the customer. Even if small, psychologically, it is reassuring to the customer to make a second purchase (after all, if the first purchase wasn't good, they would certainly not purchase again).

Often just making the prospect aware that you have other products and services may trigger them to schedule a meeting with you about them; especially if the current contract for these other items is up for renewal.

Consider also that selling the additional products and services could be more productively done from the vantage point of a strategy in your Account Management Plan.

Action Items to complete this step:

- Be prepared to cross-sell, up-sell, and add-on sell, now and in the future with this prospect.
- Identify products and services that could enhance the current sale by making what they are purchasing work better for them.
- Identify additional products and services that could be purchased by this prospect that are synergistic to the current purchase.

STRATEGIC SALES PLAN

- Determine if these add-on purchases have current or future potential.
- Identify which products and services will become a part of your Account Management Plan so that you can begin to lay the groundwork for the next Strategic Sales Plan you start for this prospective customer.

Consequences:

What are the consequences if this step is not done?

Conduct the Competitor Analyses

13. Identify your external and internal competitors.

If you plan to sell against the competition, you must know who the competition is in each sales opportunity. Can you imagine how long a professional coach would last if he/she didn't even know what team they were playing next week, much less have a game plan ready to go?

Action Items to complete this step:

- Make a list of external competitors involved in this sales opportunity. Include internal competitors such as "do nothing" and "do it internally" if they are applicable.
- List the products and services or categories of products and services in which you will be competing against in this sale.
- If there is more than one competitor for multiple products and services, you might set up a simple matrix with the products and services listed across the top and the competitors listed in the left-hand column. Wherever a competitor competes with a product or service put a checkmark to indicate the need for a competitor analysis specifically product to product or service to service.

Consequences:

What are the consequences if this step is not done?

STRATEGIC SALES PLAN

14. Conduct the competitor analyses.

The competitor analysis is the cornerstone of competitive selling. You must have at least three Unique Selling Points (USPs) that can quantifiably help the prospect meet their needs better than your competitors can, or you become a commodity where price and delivery are the primary differentiators.

Without USPs your ability to establish customer loyalty is only as good as the next price decrease you can provide.

Use the "Differentiating Factors" list in the back of the book to help you find other areas where you may have strengths. The items on this list are used by companies that sell commodities to quantifiably differentiate themselves in their marketplaces.

Action items to complete this step:

- Conduct or update the competitor analysis for each of your competitors in this sales opportunity. Look not only at your competitor's product and service but also how they do business.
- Identify your competitor's strengths by answering the question, "Why do customers buy from them?" The competitor's strengths will become your objections.
- Determine how you can neutralize their strengths by providing something that's the same or better to neutralize the objections. If not, you'll deal with them as an "unanswerable objections."
- Identify the competitor's weaknesses.
- Identify your corresponding strengths to each of the competitor's weaknesses. These now become your **Unique Selling Points (USPs)** in this sales opportunity against this competitor.

Consequences:

What are the consequences if this step is not done?

Conduct the Competitor Analyses

15. Update your list of Unique Selling Points.

In this step, you are updating the list of standard Unique Selling Points (USPs) you identified in Step 2 with those you identified after doing the competitor analysis.

You will use the USPs' in the Features, Advantages, and Benefits format throughout the steps to establish value where, in the end, they will become part of the formal or informal specifications package defining this sales opportunity.

Features, Advantages, and Benefits (FABs)

Features are the characteristics of a product, service or company that provide the Advantages and Benefits for the customer.
Advantages meet Functional Needs and explain how the characteristic (Feature) is a better way to deliver Benefits.
Benefits meet Business and Human Needs.

For example:

F Plastic containers
A Won't rust
B Minimize rusty container replacement budget

The terms, Specifications, Criteria, Requirements, Objectives, Expectations, Conditions, Objectives, and Standards can usually be used interchangeably during the sales process.

Action items to complete this step:

- Determine which of your Unique Selling Points each decision maker would have the highest level of interest in based on the role they have in the organization.
- Convert your USPs into Features, Advantages, and Benefits (FABs)

- Convert your FABs into generic topics of conversation so they can be easily brought up in discussion with minimal explanation or confusion.
    - For example, (F) plastic containers (A) won't rust (B), so you minimize the replacement budget. Convert this to "materials that won't rust."
- Use terms that make it easy to set your Unique Selling Points as specifications or criteria for making a product, service, and supplier selection.

Consequences:

What are the consequences if this step is not done?

Conduct the Competitor Analyses

16. Identify potential objections.

Customer perceived competitor strengths are a primary source of the objections you get. Industry and company reputation can also provide a few objections for you to prepare to prevent, preempt, or respond.

Determine which objections you can neutralize directly using your equal or better capability. For example, if they are a large organization with lots of resources and you are too, then it's a wash. Just be sure to let the prospect know.

If, however, it's not a wash, then you'll need to treat it as an "unanswerable objection" and use the tradeoff negotiation tactic where you offer your USPs in exchange for the customer perceived competitor strength you can't neutralize.

For example,
- *"That's true; they do have that. However, when you compare the two on ____ USP, ____, USP, and ____ USP, which would make the greatest contribution to achieving your goals."*
- *"It comes down to choosing between this and that." Which would work better for you?"*
- *"You can either get this, or you can get that, that, and the other thing (USPs) which seem to fit perfectly with where your business plan is taking you."*

Objections occur when one or more of the ten "Buyer Beliefs" are missing or weak. For example, if the prospect doesn't believe they need what you sell, you'll get objections such as "don't need it," "already have someone," or "not interested."

The essential Buyer Beliefs are:

They must believe that:
1. A **need exists**.
2. They have or share the **responsibility** to fill the need.

25

Strategic Sales Plan

3. They have or share the **authority** to fill the need.
4. The unfulfilled need is causing some **discomfort**.
5. The need has **priority** over other needs.
6. Your **type of solution** will fill the need.
7. You, your company and product/service have the **capability and credibility** to fill the need.
8. Your solution to the exclusion of competing solutions is the **best solution**.
9. The price for the solution is less than the value to be received creating a **return on investment**.
10. Your **plan for implementation** will be successful.

Usually, the current supplier (your competitor) owns many of these beliefs with the prospect. The competitor's strengths tell you which ones they own.

Once you prevent, preempt and respond to each objection identified to be caused by your competitor, your industry, and your company, then the question becomes, "you're the same so why change? This is where your Unique Selling Points come in to play to quantifiably differentiate you with this prospect.

Action items to complete this step:

- List the competitor's strengths as potential objections and how you will neutralize each one with something you offer that's equal or better.
- List any other common objections you usually deal with based on your industry, company reputation, or from any other source.
- Develop your strategies to PREVENT these objections from entering the prospect's mind by ensuring the related Buyer Beliefs are established at the right time in the sales process.
- Develop your strategies to PREEMPT these objections when it's convenient for you.
- Develop your strategies to RESPOND to those objections that could not be prevented or preempted.

Conduct the Competitor Analyses

- Prepare to use the tradeoff negotiation tactic for the unanswerable objections.

GO / NO GO

Consequences:

What are the consequences if this step is not done?

Establish the Value of What You Sell

17. Prevent, preempt, and respond to potential objections.

In Step 16 you developed the strategies to handle all the objections. In this step, you are defining "when" you will deal with them and then actually handling them. You will carry out the actions of this step throughout the sales process.

Action Items to complete this step:

- Know where and when in the sales process you will handle the objections.
- Neutralize those objections where your competitor is strong, and you have equal or better capabilities.
- Prevent, preempt, and respond to all remaining objections.
- Negotiate the "Unanswerable Objections" using the "tradeoff" negotiation tactic.

Consequences:

What are the consequences if this step is not done?

Establish the Value of What You Sell

18. Focus the topics of conversation on your Unique Selling Points (USPs).

This is the step where you use the list of all the Unique Selling Points (USPs) you developed (standards and new ones from the competitor analysis updates). You also converted your FABs to generic or general topics. You will use those in this step.

Your competitor analysis will always tell you where your strengths are where your competitor is weak. Your research of the prospect's business will tell you where you'll find the probable needs.

You are now moving out of the research phase of selling and beginning to implement your competitive sales strategy which is to open the sales interaction by orienting the prospect to areas where you are strong, your competitor is weak, and the customer has needs.

Examples:

- *From our tour of the facility, I can see where you've got people scrubbing rust stains and moving product from rusting containers to new ones. What are the other challenges with this process we should address?*
- *Based on what I've learned so far there are three areas I'd like to focus on; __ (USP), __ (USP) and __ (USP), which of these would you like to talk about first?*
- *I talked with ____ yesterday, and s/he indicated that __ (USP) is something that needs to be addressed. Could you tell me more about this?*
- *Could you tell me more about the specific process you use to ___?* (Note this could also be a Research Question).
- *In thinking about ___, what are your greatest concerns?* (Note this question combines the orientation with the next step Symptom Question).

29

Strategic Sales Plan

Action items to complete this step:

- Develop opening remarks in the form of questions that will focus the conversation to explore the prospect's priority areas of need where you are strong, and your competitor is weak.
- Zero in on specific areas that will lead to the discovery of other problems you can solve with your USPs.
- Select the five USP areas with the highest probability of differentiating you from the competitors, have the greatest value and are the easiest to quantify with the decision maker with whom you're meeting.

Consequences:

What are the consequences if this step is not done?

Establish the Value of What You Sell

19. Identify the signs caused by your USPs' missing Advantages and Benefits.

The signs and symptoms to look for are the missing Advantages and Benefits provided by your Unique Selling Point's Feature. For example, suppose you sell a container that is made of plastic to replace one made of steel that has significant problems with rust.

From the earlier example, the symptoms you would see could include rust on containers, rust stains where they're stored, containers in poor condition, replacement budget, and so on. Those are the clues or signs and symptoms that they have a problem with rusting containers.

Examples:

- *What are your greatest concerns about using containers that rust?*
- *When it comes to _____* (missing Advantages and Benefits of USP), *what are your greatest areas of concern?*
- *How often are you seeing __ or __ (missing Advantages and Benefits)?*
- *What about _____ gives you the biggest headaches?*
- *What takes up most of your time with _____ ?*
- *Where's the pain?*
- *What could be gained if this _____ was no-longer an issue?*

Action items to complete this step:

- List what you'd see if the Advantages and Benefits provided by your Unique Selling Point's Feature are not present. This is how you identify the signs, symptoms, and clues that suggest a prospect needs your USP.

- Begin to move the prospect out of his/her comfort zone by asking the questions to get the decision-maker to realize they don't have the Advantages and Benefits.
- Uncover the hidden needs not being met by the competitor (your USPs).
- Prevent the prospect from denying a problem exists.
- Preempt or answer the prospect's/customer's question, "What makes you think I've got a problem?"

Consequences:

What are the consequences if this step is not done?

Establish the Value of What You Sell

20. Confirm the problems caused by the missing USPs.

Define the problems as the missing Features that provide the Advantages and Benefits that are showing themselves as signs and symptoms because they too are missing. This is circular logic, and that makes it irrefutable.

If the prospect has rust stains (sign) caused by the use of metal containers, then the problem is one of "not having" containers made of a material (like plastic) that won't rust. This also points the problem to a solution.

Examples:

- *The problem is not using a material like plastic for your containers, isn't it?*
- *This could be a problem with not having _____ (state your Feature in generic terms).*
- *What do you think is causing what we're seeing here?*
- *That could be a problem, couldn't it?*
- *That sounds like a problem worth exploring further, doesn't it?*
- *That's a problem we've seen before, and it can be pretty costly so let's dig a little deeper into it* (now ask a quantifying question *–How often do you think this is happening?*

Action Items to complete this step:

- Identify and get agreement on the root-cause of the symptoms.
- Confirm the existence of problems.
- Define the problem as one you can solve with a unique selling point.

STRATEGIC SALES PLAN

- Define the problem, or potential problem, as one that may lead to the development of a modified or new product or service.

Consequences:

What are the consequences if this step is not done?

Establish the Value of What You Sell

21. Quantify their costs of not having your USPs to establish the value of the solution.

Unless you know the value to the customer of what you're selling, it will be very difficult to sell value.

All **value selling models** use questions to quantify and establish the value of what's being sold using the prospect's facts and figures. These calculations or "Cost-Benefit Analysis" are often done by quantifying what it costs the prospect in the past, present, and the future not to have your Unique Selling Points. Costs can be subjective, emotional, and financial.

Include in your calculations the "cost to use" the competitor's product or service as well as any "hidden costs" (competitor's weaknesses) associated with the supplier they choose. Adding these together would result in the "bottom-line" costs or the total cost of ownership versus price which is the "top-line" cost.

Price pressure can be reduced or eliminated if you will help the prospect cost justify the unique capabilities you're offering to solve the problems. You have to help them with the cost-benefit analysis because they don't know your unique capabilities the way you do.

If you don't help them, they won't be able to justify to themselves or their boss, your higher price (top-line), or justify the hassle of changing suppliers.

What is this problem costing them? What will it cost them over the next 12 months (or length of contract or useful life of the product) if they don't fix it by getting your USPs? Future costs, if real, must show up in their budgets somewhere.

Sometimes the decision maker doesn't know the numbers. To keep the momentum going and prevent the sale from stalling, you can always use industry standards or norms. You do this by stating the standard and then asking if they would see their actual numbers being a little higher or a little lower than the industry norms. Whatever you get, nail it down as an educated guess and move on. You'll validate it in a later step.

Examples:

- *How often does that happen?*
- *What kinds of costs are involved?*
- *How many people, for how long, at what rate?*
- *What does that mean over the next 12 months?*
- *There's not a lot we can do to make up for the current costs, but the quicker we're able to move forward, the sooner we can put that money to better use elsewhere.*
- *What effect does that have on your ability to meet your production goals?*

Action items to complete this step:

- List each of the problems the prospect has admitted to having in the previous step (and throughout the process).
- Identify the potential costs (past, present, and future) to the prospect if the problem is not solved. Use the prospect's facts and figures.
- Quantify financially, subjectively (hassle), and emotionally (frustrations).
- ASK don't tell. Ask what it costs them not to have the Advantages and Benefits (now and in the future) of your USP's Feature?
- Identify what it "costs to use" the product or service. For example, miles per gallon, accuracy rate, risk insurance, or whatever applies to what you sell.
- Cast these numbers into the reasonable future such as the length of the agreement or useful life of the product.
- Focus on the true bottom-line value or total cost of ownership, which includes the "cost to get" plus the "cost to use" along with any "hidden costs" (competitor's weaknesses) to find the money in the budget. It's there but just called something else.

Establish the Value of What You Sell

- Establish the basis to determine the customer's return on investment.
- Prevent or minimize "price" and "stall" type objections.
- Create a sense of urgency and put the pressure of time on the customer by quantifying the consequences of not solving the problems with your unique selling points.
- Use Standards of Legitimacy (industry norms) where numbers are not available to keep up the momentum and to prevent the sale from stalling at this point.
- Quantify enough value for what you sell so that if your competitor drops their price by 30%, you would still have sufficient value quantified to counter that number.

Consequences:

What are the consequences if this step is not done?

22. Set your USPs as specifications that must be met to solve the problems.

Specifications are identified and set to ensure the solutions they buy will solve the problem and do away with the associated costs.

In more formal, complex, or large purchases, these specifications are written. You want to make sure that your Unique Selling Points are included in these specifications or selection criteria.

If your competitor can't meet this new set of specifications, which they can't if they include your USPs, then their competitive position is severely weakened.

What fully quantified USPs can you set as part of the specification package during this step?

Note that the terms criteria, objectives, requirements, specifications, conditions, expectations, standards, and other similar terms are essentially interchangeable.

Examples:

- *Given the challenges and costs, it seems that one of your minimum specifications would be to start using containers that won't rust. That'll clear up a lot of issues, won't it?*
- *One requirement that would have to be met when selecting a supplier would be _____ (USP FAB). Is that about how you see it?*
- *One of the primary objectives that you want to accomplish would be _____ (referencing unique capability).*
- *Another area we talked about that seems more of a nice to have if we can get it rather than a hard, fast*

Establish the Value of What You Sell

specification is ____ (USP), is that pretty much where we are with that one?

Action items to complete this step:

- Define, set, and agree on the requirements that must be met to solve the identified problems.
- Include your unique selling points in the specifications to help the prospect rule out the competition.
- Focus attention on solutions.

Consequences:

What are the consequences if this step is not done?

STRATEGIC SALES PLAN

23. Competitor Proof with Benefits Questions.

The only way you can know which of the many benefits you can offer are the ones that will motivate these decision makers to take action to buy is to ask!

By asking the Benefits questions you create attitudes, prevent skepticism type objections, competitor proof the prospect, and discover personal value. The person who makes the claims about Benefits has the burden of proof.

Ask each decision maker about the Benefits they will get that will apply to themselves and apply to other decision makers as well.

Asking is a great way to help them rehearse defenses so they can run interference for you and sell internally for you to cover the decision makers you can't reach.

Asking the Benefits Questions is also how you change bias from neutral to favorable to champion.

Examples:

- *In addition to what we've talked about, what other benefits do you see getting?*
- *Why would your staff favor this change?*
- *How would the salespeople see this move on your part?*
- *Why would your customers' customers' like this change?*
- *Who else would benefit from doing this?*
- *What would ____ get from this?*
- *Why would ____ support you?*
- *How does this fit with your company's strategic initiative to reduce costs and improve profitability?*
- *What about the Finance department, what benefits would they see from having your criteria met?*

Establish the Value of What You Sell

- *What other value would your team get from with this plan?*

Action items to complete this step:

- Ask each decision maker about the benefits they believe they will get from each USP set as criteria so you can discover true buying motives important to each of them.
- Ask each decision maker you interview about benefits they think others (especially those you can't get in to interview) will get so you can rehearse them to sell internally for you when you are not around, and so you can cover decision makers you can't meet with during this sales cycle.
- Ask so you can rehearse the decision maker to defend the criteria and turn changeable beliefs into resistant attitudes to create Champions and to competitor proof the decision makers.
- Ask; don't tell them the benefits, so they make the claims for benefits to be received, rather than you making them. The person making the claims has the burden of proof.

Consequences:

What are the consequences if this step is not done?

STRATEGIC SALES PLAN

24. Complete the interviews with key decision makers.

Each decision-maker will make a different type of decision about your ability to meet their needs. Therefore, each decision-maker must be interviewed or covered in some way so they can be on your side.

Review the organization chart you completed earlier. Be alert to others who seem not to be directly involved with the decision making but who can have a significant influence on the outcome (decision maker's boss, a new person to the party, rising star, political influencer, etc.).

Action items to complete this step:

- Update your checklist of internal and external influences and decision makers to ensure that you don't miss anyone who could impact the sale.
- Cross check decision-making process with the prospect's organizational chart.
- Review your master list of decision makers to ensure all that can be interviewed or covered, have been.
- Place a checkmark in the appropriate box when each role has been interviewed or covered.
- List any additional decision makers to interview and schedule the appointments to do so within the sales cycle.

GO / NO GO

Consequences:

What are the consequences if this step is not done?

25. Validate any cost-benefit data that used industry standards.

Since doing cost-benefit analysis often involves using "standards of legitimacy" or mutually acceptable averages for the industry, it may become important to determine the "real" numbers for the prospect using his/her facts and figures if at all possible.

Industry norms might get challenged during a proposal or presentation. However, if the "real" numbers are confidential, then use and note the industry standards or norms are being used. You provide the formulas, and they provide the numbers during their internal decision-making meetings.

Action items to complete this step:

- Identify any cost-benefit data that is yet to be confirmed.
- Validate or provide the formulas to validate any cost-benefit data that used standards of legitimacy, industry norms, or any other standards rather than the prospect's facts and figures.
- Validate subjective or emotional costs. For example, confirm the percent of people annoyed, frustrated, or stressed and the related costs such as turnover, poor work performance (low morale), risk management costs, or medical expenses.

Consequences:

What are the consequences if this step is not done?

Complete the Logistics Steps

26. Advise and get agreement on the next steps to advance the sale.

Who must do what, when, how, with what resources, in what time frame, with what feedback loops occurring at what milestones to advance the sale?

You most likely know the steps that must be carried out for the prospect to own your product/service. However, not every company buys in the same way.

The purpose of this step is to learn the prospect's logistical buying process and to confirm any "soft" data you gathered along the way.

And, since you've gotten this far, it's time to carefully review the previous 25 steps in your Strategic Sales Plan to make sure nothing was overlooked, each step was done completely and is firmly locked into place.

Action items to complete this step:

- List and confirm the steps the prospect must take in order to purchase your products/services in this sale that are in addition to those identified in your strategic sales plan.
- Develop a written interim action plan to:
    o Demonstrate, in writing, your commitment to do what you say you are going to do.
    o Get a commitment, in writing, from your prospect to carry out the action items that would advance the sale.
    o Block the competition between calls.

Complete the Logistics Steps

- o Monitor and document performance against the strategic sales plan.
- o Demonstrate organization and clear direction to advancing the sale.
- o Weaken current competitor's position.
- Identify any other buying influences which might influence the sale.
- Add these additional buyer influences to your master list and to the Account Management Plan.

Consequences:

What are the consequences if this step is not done?

27. Outline feedback loops, milestones, measurements, and follow-up process.

Sometimes there are significant costs involved with providing certain types of feedback and measurement; particularly when you take the frequency of these items into account. For many types of product and services, there are rewards and penalties for hitting or not hitting the milestones according to plan.

Identify who needs to know what's going on during product and service delivery. Try to get critical decision-makers on your feedback list. Include both internal and external customers. Add these people to your master list of contacts and include them in your Account Management Plan as appropriate.

Detail the feedback loops: *Who needs to know what? Any costs associated with providing the information?*
Define the milestones: *What are they and what do they mean? Any penalties or rewards attached to meeting or not meeting them?*
Identify Measurements: *What are they, who will take them, how often will they be made, who will receive them, how will they be used, and who will pay for them?*
List Follow-Up Process: *Any other official follow-up expected? What frequency, methods, and costs?*

Action items to complete this step:

- Determine who is expecting what type of feedback during the process and when.
- Identify the milestones for product/service delivery and whether there are penalties and rewards associated.
- Specify any measurements, how they will be taken, and how they will be used.
- Specify the follow-up process including who will be involved doing what, when, at what cost, and who will

Complete the Logistics Steps

pay for anything outside of your normal account management process.
- Add this information to your Plan for Implementation step in your Customer Value Proposition. Add the people identified in this step to your master list of contacts and your Account Management Plan.

Consequences:

What are the consequences if this step is not done?

28. Develop product/service delivery phase-in plans.

Be prepared to present in detail how you plan to implement your products and services.

Note any safeguards, redundancies, and other mechanisms that will enable the process of implementation to "self-correct" along the way. Identifying these will significantly reduce anxieties that might lead to cold feet or cause the buyers to stay with what they know (the current system and supplier).

Identify optional target dates for implementation. Always work against the clock. Psychologically it plants the seed of accomplishing a goal. Goals without deadlines lack urgency. Get the prospect to agree to at least a "target" date.

Determine ideal starting dates to meet target dates. This step helps you increase the sense of urgency of getting started. It may be very real that if the selection decision gets delayed, they might not meet their timeline of filling their needs. Work backward from the target date for implementation to lay out the action items that must be done to meet it.

Action items to complete this step:

- Develop product and service delivery phase-in plans.
- Agree on target dates for implementation.
- Agree on ideal starting dates to meet target dates.
- Consider all the steps that must be completed and the amount of time it will take including getting the contract or agreement signed.

Consequences:

What are the consequences if this step is not done?

Complete the Logistics Steps

29. Determine product/service availability.

Many companies have limits to their capacity to produce products and deliver services. By the time you get to this step, you must become aware of any limitations you might face. If there are any, you may need to revisit the previous step to make sure you can meet delivery expectations.

How you plan to structure the sale, pricing issues, delivery methods and so on may require internal (your company) approvals.

Action items to complete this step:

- Determine your company's capability to deliver within the agreed upon target dates.
- Who in your company must sign-off on this sale? Get the key players in your organization on-line early in the process. Develop a checklist of these individuals and let them know about this pending sale.
- Be sure you are prepared to sell this project internally. What benefits will the key players in your company receive as a result of this project?
- Are there any obstacles that will need to be handled internally so that you are capable of meeting delivery?
- Obtain any internal (your company) approvals as needed.
- Confirm that you're capable of performing to specifications.

GO / NO GO

Consequences:

What are the consequences if this step is not done?

30. Complete required pre-purchase approvals.

Pre-purchase approvals include a wide range of items from beta tests and pilot studies to having the right type and amount of insurance or staff with the right credentials.

For international business, it may mean completing certain government documents, or it may mean getting a local partner.

Other approvals could include an evaluation of your quality process, completing a vendor application, meeting insurance or bonding requirements, acquiring financing. They could also include assuring environmental compliance, being under pre-set OSHA recordable accident levels, documenting safety training, providing technical and performance references, maintaining certain organizational memberships, possessing critical certifications, and a whole host of other types of pre-approvals. Know which are required for your business to become an approved vendor.

Action items to complete this step:

- Identify and list any pre-purchase approvals are required for your business to become an approved or pre-approved vendor.
- Identify and assign who will complete what action, when it will be done, and how you'll know it's been done.
- Coordinate getting pre-approvals needed with the timelines established for product/service phase-in plans.
- Record when it is completed and how it was delivered to the prospect (You'll often be chasing these documents down).
- Record the feedback you have received from the pre-purchase approvals.
- Take any corrective action required. Record who, when, and where it was sent.

Complete the Logistics Steps

- Keep track of completion and follow-up dates on those yet to be done or yet to receive feedback on those completed by your company.

GO / NO GO

Consequences:

What are the consequences if this step is not done?

STRATEGIC SALES PLAN

31. Exchange any additional data, specifications, or financial information.

Additional data could range from getting or confirming billing and shipping addresses to critical drawings, specifications, terms and conditions, or scope of work statements.

Financial and credit information may be a part of the previous pre-approval process, or it may not come until you're submitting your proposal. But, for many companies (and some entire industries), getting or giving financing is a separate significant step upon which the entire sale is based.

Action items to complete this step:

- Manage the process of information exchange.
- List any additional information that is not a part of the pre-approval process but must be exchanged to advance this sale.
- Note the source of the information and if it is completed.
- Clear any missing information hurdles.
- Clarify, confirm, and provide, any financial information required from your company.
- Clarify, confirm, and receive, any financial information required from the prospect's company.

Consequences:

What are the consequences if this step is not done?

Complete the Logistics Steps

32. Identify and prepare your Recommenders to be your Champions.

This step is often done as a part of the pre-approval process but does come up later as well, either on its own as represented here, or as part of awarding the contract where the final step is to check your references.

Although most buyers will ask you to provide three references, it's not uncommon for them to contact people from your customer list as well or to contact someone they know who is using your products/services. This is another reason to make sure you are carefully following your Account Management Plans with your customers.

Pay particular attention to those Recommenders who can support a point that you've made where the prospect didn't seem totally convinced. When you prepare them, let them know to emphasize those areas. For example, they could then say, *"Our salesperson_____ (your name) told me you had a particular interest in how _____ is working. Let me tell you that _____ . . ."*

Action items to complete this step:

- Prepare external Recommenders to address prospect's specific areas of concern.
- Prepare internal Champions to support your efforts and to cover the decision makers you weren't able to reach.

Consequences:

What are the consequences if this step is not done?

53

Propose, Present, and Negotiate

33. Prepare and submit the Customer Value Proposition (CVP).

The Customer Value Proposition (CVP) follows a specific format to demonstrate how your company, product, and service will meet the prospect's requirements (that now include your Unique Selling Points - USPs).

Additionally, there are several psychological principles involved to help break any irrational customer loyalty bond, create a balanced thinking strategy on costs and pricing, keep the pressure of time and sense of urgency on the prospective customer's shoulders, and accommodate both ends of the personality based decision-making continuum.

In most standard proposals, the seller uses the first section to state their credentials, and it's all about them. However, that's not what the prospect is interested in at this time. It's not about you; it's about them. So, establish your credibility with the first step in the CVP, the Situational Analysis. Put your credentials at the end like you would in a press release.

Action items to complete this step:

- **Situational Analysis:** Present your understanding of the situation. Demonstrate knowledge of the prospect's organization and situation to establish trust and rapport.
- **Value (Economic and Other Impact):** Quantify the seriousness of the problems the prospect is faced with to help build the business case for moving forward with the purchase. Use their facts and figures in this step.
- **Selection Criteria:** List product, service, company selection specifications in the left-hand column (one

item per row) and how you will meet them in the right-hand column.
- **Investment and Financial Comparison Analysis:** The financial investment can be presented in a "balance sheet" style format to show the comparison between current costs and future costs or you can use a straight listing of prices. Clarify any competitor equivalency issues, e.g., they have ten bottles per case, and you have 12 which could show them to have a lower price per case.
- **Plan for Implementation:** Present the plan of action and within the first five to seven steps ensure that one action item complete, one that will complete without input from the prospect, and one step that provides feedback. This strategy will satisfy both ends of the personality continuum that relates to decision-making styles.

Consequences:

What are the consequences if this step is not done?

34. Conduct sales presentation using the CVP format.

Presentations can range from a very informal discussion during a conference call to a very formal presentation in which you could use handouts, flipcharts, whiteboard, or slides.

The people attending from the prospect's company could be those decision makers you interviewed or decision makers who were not on the list.

The good news is that you were able to rehearse the decision makers to move to the Favorable and perhaps Champion levels of bias so that they can defend and sell for you during the presentation if needed.

You'll want to know who will attend from the prospect's company and their decision-making role so you can direct the correct Benefit statements (and questions) to them.

Make sure the roles for members of your presentation team are very clear. Anyone violating boundaries will put the presentation at risk, as well as, diminish the credibility of the person whose role it is to handle those questions. The presentation leader can re-direct questions to anyone on the team and then take the lead back after the answer.

Action items to complete this step:

- Identify attendees and roles from the prospect's company.
- Identify and clarify roles and boundaries of members of your presenting team.
- Conduct the presentation based on the Customer Value Proposition format.
- During the Plan for Implementation step, have at least one action item complete, one that will complete without

Propose, Present, and Negotiate

input from the prospect, and one step that provides feedback.

Consequences:

What are the consequences if this step is not done?

Strategic Sales Plan

35. Prospect affirms your ability to meet the criteria.

This step could lead directly to the purchase order or contract as it stands or it could require minor mutually agreeable items to modify.

In other instances, they may want to negotiate or renegotiate some portions of your proposal. This will be the topic of the next step.

In any case, you'll want to start the implementation phase that can occur without risk or cost prior to getting a contract.

Action items to complete this step:

- Implement the steps from your Plan of Implementation that do not require the prospect's approval.
- Get internal permissions as needed to make minor modifications.
- Provide ample feedback to the decision-making team about the progress on these steps.
- Time these actions within the pre-defined schedule developed during your product and service delivery phase-in plans.

GO / NO GO

Consequences:

What are the consequences if this step is not done?

36. Conclude final negotiations.

You engage in negotiations throughout the sales process. Some are big, and some are small. The big ones usually occur after the presentation. This is where the prospect sees that you can meet their needs better than the competition and now wants to negotiate item by item to make each more agreeable to their organization.

Negotiations are not one-way. This is also your opportunity to get what you need from them so you can accommodate the changes they would like you to make.

Most sales negotiations center around price. To prevent or minimize price negotiations, you must carry out the steps to establish the value of your Unique Selling Points and how they enhance the overall value of what you sell. If you don't, the prospect won't understand the value they will lose by not selecting your offer.

Even worse, they will view and treat what you sell as a commodity. That means they will have more options to choose from which then leads to pressure for the best price, delivery, and other terms.

As you prepare for the negotiations, keep in mind that difficult or adversarial style negotiations can be exhausting and leave the prospect too burned-out to make any change, and in fact, they may turn the prospect off for doing business with you ("If this is what it's like just trying to business with you, forget it.").

Action items to complete this step:

- Conduct the negotiations using a win-win principled negotiations style.
- Mentally prepare by reviewing your past negotiation successes, your credentials, and the value of the Unique Selling Points you bring to the negotiations.

- Jointly set the agenda using general objective style statements you're both interested in achieving.
- Find the Functional, Business, and Human Needs motivating the requested changes for all parties involved.
- Understand the limits, risks, rewards, and options for all parties in the negotiations.
- Use the trade-off negotiations strategy to avoid hitting limits.
- Diplomatically counter adversarial tactics.
- Use "consensus building" methods throughout the negotiations.
- Negotiate the standards that create the results, not the results themselves.
- Never give in to pressure; only to principle, e.g., larger volume or longer agreement could mean lower costs and that could mean lower price.
- Focus on the fairness principle. Negotiations should lead to a feeling that the outcome was "fair" for all involved.
- Feel good about the negotiations or stop and regroup.
- Keep in mind your future working relationship. Use ego strengthening statements and actions to create positive momentum.

Consequences:

What are the consequences if this step is not done?

37. Final budget approval received.

Getting final budget approval is just one more step you listed in the "Plan for Implementation" section of your CVP.

Sometimes you know the approval has cleared when you get the contract to sign and sometimes, it's just another point of negotiations.

If you don't get it on schedule, then do some diagnostic checking of previous steps in this Strategic Sales Plan to make sure everything you've done is on target.

Action items to complete this step:

- Check to see if you've created enough value to keep the sense of urgency high.
- Check with your coaches to make sure everything is still on track.
- Be aware of external events that affect the prospect's company.
- Meet with the prospect to identify what's slowing down their internal final approvals.
- Reset delivery timelines as necessary.

GO / NO GO

Consequences:

What are the consequences if this step is not done?

STRATEGIC SALES PLAN

38. Contract signed, or letter of engagement received.

For many products or services or more complex delivery systems, some form of written agreement is often required to clarify who is responsible for doing what, when, how, in what time frame, and at what cost.

The written component of this step could range from a legal contract, a written agreement, to a letter of engagement, a letter of confirmation, a scope of work, to a simple receipt with the terms and conditions on it, and so on.

In some instances, the contract itself is a major part of the negotiations. In any case, you want something in writing that spells out the requirements so that both buyer and seller know what to expect.

Action items to complete this step:

- If possible, your company should write the final contract or agreement to be sent to the prospect. That way your terms and conditions are sure to be included.
- Once you get the modified contract from the prospect, review it carefully for any discrepancies using your negotiation notes.
- Alert the prospect, now a customer, that the agreement has been signed and is on its way to them.
- Be aware that this process of getting both sides to sign may take longer than you think. Adjust your schedule accordingly.

Consequences:

What are the consequences if this step is not done?

Propose, Present, and Negotiate

39. Customer notifies current supplier(s).

If the customer has current suppliers who lost the sale, they will often need to notify them before you can begin work. For some products, they may need to transition work components, data, inventory, and so on to you. Diplomacy is important.

A sale can stall at this point because the decision-maker doesn't know how to break the news to the supplier that they lost the account. This could be a sensitive time because the competitor might take desperate and drastic steps to keep the sale.

Examples of desperate and drastic "save the sale" tactics:

- Price drop – competitor drops price too big for the prospect to ignore
- Buyer's boss – competitor leveraging friendships
- Political pressure – competitor lobbying decision makers
- Negative selling sabotage – competitor talking about how sad it is, going to miss you, just a few lousy bucks, etc.
- Me too – competitor now claims they can do everything you can do and do it better

Examples of methods to "cement the sale:"

- List and assign notification of prospect decision-makers between you, your team and the buyer.
- Involve buyer's boss. Send an immediate "thank you" note to the Decision Makers from your boss or your boss's boss (same number to same number).
- Meet with as many people you'll be working with as you can and announce that you're the new supplier. Shake hands, smile, and be warm and enthusiastic.
- Implement major step(s) in the plan for implementation to make it extremely difficult to turn back the clock.
- Ask for Internal/External Referrals.

Strategic Sales Plan

Action Items to complete this step:

- Determine how and when the buyer will notify the competition.
- Prepare for potential tactics the competitor might implement to overturn your sale:
- List the steps you and the buyer will do to cement the sale:
- Take these and other actions that will make it incredibly difficult for the decision makers to go back on their announcement.

Consequences:

What are the consequences if this step is not done?

Deliver Your Products & Services

40. Identify and arrange to meet the critical support people.

These are the decision influences that will have an agenda if your company is selected.

These people provide support for the delivery of your product or service. For example, if you are holding a conference at a hotel, the catering staff that sets up your room and makes sure your materials get there could make or break your presentation.

If your product deliveries arrive after the plant closes, security personnel, if they don't cooperate, could make your deliveries late. If you need access to secure locations in the customer's facilities, you'll need clearances and credentials. If you sell software, you may train the End Users as well, but if those who install it don't do a good job, you're the person who will end up with a black eye.

Decision makers' assistants, secretaries, and other support staff can make a big difference in your ability to move smoothly about the organization.

Note however that these individuals are not the End Users who will actually use your products/services. They will be further identified in the next step.

Action Items to complete this step:

- Identify additional support people that could influence the sale now, impact performance, or impact your ability to win repeat business.

- Add these people to your list of contacts for account management activities as needed.

Consequences:

What are the consequences if this step is not done?

Deliver Your Products & Services

41. Identify specific End Users involved in the project.

Very often, you will not meet or talk to the End Users until you are deeply involved in the sales process or until after the contract is moving forward.

You can find yourself at a significant competitive disadvantage if your competitor builds and leverages their relationships with the End Users and you don't. The End Users can certainly ask that the previous supplier get the opportunity to regain the business because they like working with them.

So much of this sale (and future ones) hinges on how well you, product/service, and company are received by the End Users.

Action Items to complete this step:

- Meet, engage, and build a positive relationship with the End Users for your products and services.
- Create coaches and mentors.
- Include End Users in the product and service delivery "quality check" step (Step 42).
- Add contacts to your Account Management Plan as needed.

Consequences:

What are the consequences if this step is not done?

STRATEGIC SALES PLAN

42. Conduct quality checks of the product and service delivery.

Quality is defined as "conformance to requirements."

Look at the list of specifications or requirements you and your customer agree to for the purchase. If you meet them, you are delivering a quality product and service.

You want to meet the requirements, not exceed them. Exceeding them may cause the customer to think their paying for more than they need.

Expectations are different. Exceeding their expectations in how the product and service are being delivered will "wow" them.

For example, the restaurant cooks can just put the food on your plate to meet the requirements of what you ordered, or they could carefully arrange it, perhaps add a flower, or a swirl of some sauce to make a beautiful presentation of your meal. Same money but with a little artistic flair and the customer's expectations have been exceeded.

You've no doubt heard the saying; "under promise and over deliver." Live it. It's not hard to do. It costs you so little to add a ribbon to the box, a shine to the product, and a smile to providing a service. Sometimes it can be just you paying attention to every detail and providing excellent account management.

If there is a non-conformance discovered during your quality inspection, then your service recovery actions must simply overwhelm the customer. Nothing short of this will prevent the customer from thinking and feeling they might have made a mistake. Overwhelming them with responsiveness will make them feel good about having chosen you and your company.

Deliver Your Products & Services

Action Items to complete this step:

- Get the list of product and service delivery requirements to ensure these are being met.
- Ask, how can we make that a bit better?
- Plan and implement the "wow" factor to exceed their expectations.
- Overwhelm with service recovery efforts if needed.
- Define and measure customer satisfaction.

Consequences:

What are the consequences if this step is not done?

Manage Your Account

43. Implement sales activities to competitor proof and grow the account.

68-82% of all customers go away due to neglect or an attitude of indifference being expressed to them by someone in your company. Poor follow up can be seen the same way when it comes time to renew the account for the next contract period.

There are many activities you'll need to do to manage this account.

First order of business is to **competitor proof** your new account. There are several ways to do this including:

1. **Get an add-on sale:** The logic is that they wouldn't buy from you again if the first sale were a mistake. This add-on sale is psychologically reassuring to them. It can be a small thing, just do it as quickly as is prudent after the first sale is complete.
2. **Create attitudes favorable to you:** The Benefit questions will do this nicely. For example, *"What's most impressive about how this is working for you? Why do you like that? What about your manager, what does s/he like?"* Gently challenging (asking why they like something) the person's belief about what they like evokes the defense emotions. Once the belief and the emotion become attached to each other, it becomes an attitude which is resistant to change. Competitors will have an exceptionally hard time made worse for them if they ask the prospect "why" they like or want your USPs.
3. **Obtain testimonials:** Again, they are now justifying and defending themselves why they chose you.

Manage Your Account

4. **Ask them to be a reference:** Now they are justifying and defending their purchase to others.
5. **Ask for referrals:** Referred leads are significantly easier to contact and get in to see; take 30% fewer contacts to close a sale; are 60%-80% more likely to buy; will buy on average 23% more; and, are four times more likely to give additional referrals. List specific companies and individuals to whom you will ask for referrals. Narrow the scope of areas that the person can see, i.e., professional organizations, suppliers, customer groups, etc.
6. **Develop coaches, sponsors, and mentors:** This is a continual process of developing business relationships.

Next order of business is to **grow the account** through cross-selling, add-on selling, and up-selling, as well as, getting repeat business for this sale.

1. **Cross-selling:** Look for synergistic products and services you have available that would seem to fit naturally with the current purchase.
2. **Add-on selling:** These are products and services you add to the current purchase to make it better. For example, *"Would you like catsup with those fries? Would you like a new gasket with your replacement pump?"*
3. **Up-selling:** This is the same product or service but made or provided to a higher standard. For example, you could upgrade the cabin on the cruise you just purchased that would include a balcony for just a few dollars more. Or, how about getting the car with seats that have both heating and air conditioning?
4. **Repeat business:** And of course, you want to stay on top of renewing any business you currently have with the customer. The activities for making sure you're doing a quality job will go a long way toward making sure this happens.

STRATEGIC SALES PLAN

With these activities, you'll want to **time-sequence** multiple methods of contacts to get them done. Modify the guidelines below to fit what you sell.

- All key decision makers are to be contacted every 90 days.
- All key decision makers should receive a first-class letter at least twice a year.
- All key decision-makers should receive an in-person visit at least once a year.
- All non-key decision-makers should not go longer than 120 days between contacts.

❖ Write your contact plans and call-objectives for the next 90 days.
❖ Contact schedule transferred to your calendar: **YES   NO**

Your repeat contact schedule should follow that best suited for what you sell, the call-objectives you are attempting to achieve, and the demands of your territory.

Action Items to complete this step:

- Establish an effective contact schedule for each decision-maker to enable you to accomplish the contact call objectives.
- Use multiple methods of contact to maintain desired frequency levels and to minimize costs.
- Competitor proof the customer.
- Grow the account.
- Obtain repeat business.

Consequences:

What are the consequences if this step is not done?

44. Recognize the signs your account may be in trouble before it's too late.

Some studies have shown that it costs six times more to obtain a new customer than it does to keep an old one. Just looking at this Strategic Sales Plan should attest to the amount of effort that will be required on your part to get new customers, build new relationships, and so on.

It makes sense to be aware of the signs that suggest an account is in trouble. Implementing your Account Management Plan will make these clues obvious to you.

Common clues that your account is in trouble:

1. Your phone calls go unreturned.
2. You do not get a timely response to your requests.
3. You don't have a specific project underway.
4. Mindshare is decreasing.
5. The customer adds competing product lines.
6. Complaints increase, and customer satisfaction is decreasing.
7. The customer is not receiving measurable benefits.
8. The customer is relying less and less on your resources.
9. The customer is not taking advantage of training or other activities offered.
10. Contact with customers exceeds the minimal time limits you set between contacts.
11. You don't know about new decision makers or organizational changes.
12. Your access to decision makers decreases.
13. The customer asks for more and more types of services, adjustments or product/service modifications you cannot offer.
14. A slight but steady decrease in the amount and type of business you are doing with the customer.
15. Customer contacts are asking competitor comparison type questions.

STRATEGIC SALES PLAN

Action Items to complete this step:

- As a routine part of your Account Management process, review these clues that the account might be trending away from you.
- Intensify your contact schedule when you don't have a current project working or if you notice any of the common clues that your account may be in trouble.

Consequences:

What are the consequences if this step is not done?

Resources Specific to the Strategic Sales Plan

Books/Ebooks:
- Objection Free Selling: How to Prevent, Preempt, and Respond to Every Sales Objection You Get (Amazon Top 100 Best Seller)
- Value Selling Strategies P.R.O.S.P.E.C.T. Model (Amazon Top 100 Best Seller)
- Telephone Cold Calling with Voice Mail Strategies (Amazon Top 100 Best Seller)
- Profile and Qualify Sales Prospects
- Sales Prospecting: The Hunt for New Customers
- Goal Setting
- Trust and Rapport Building
- Competitor Analysis

Web-Based Training (WBT): www.SalesHelp.com
- Strategic Sales Plan
- Objection Free Selling
- Profile and Qualify Sales Prospects
- Trust and Rapport Building
- Competitor Analysis
- Features – Advantages - Benefits
- FAB – TEA Value Selling Model
- Value Selling Strategies P.R.O.S.P.E.C.T. Model

Glossary of Terms

account potential (A, B, C): Rating based on total account sales volume potential. Classify large accounts as "A" size, medium accounts as "B" potential and small accounts as "C."

active listening skills: Differentiated from passive listening as you might do while in a lecture or watching television. Actively listening means to communicate that you are hearing and understanding what is being said. These skills include acceptance responses (uh huh, I see, yes, head shaking), repeating verbatim (repeating a telephone number), paraphrasing (restating in your own words) reflecting (feeding back the emotional overtones), clarifying questions (follow up questions to ensure understanding), summarizing (repeat, paraphrase and reflect key points in summary format). Additionally, see Psychological Truth.

advantages: Explain your features in a way that tells how they are a better way of providing Benefits than the competitor's way of providing benefits. Advantages meet Functional needs which answers the question of what it does and why it's better.

agenda close: Laying out the agenda of items to be accomplished with the prospect. When the prospect agrees to the agenda, they have pre-agreed to doing each item listed. *"And so, if we work through this issue okay, then we can tackle this one, and once that's done, I think we're clear to start on the purchase order, and once that's approved, then you should start seeing these issues clear up in a week. How does that sound to you?"* If the prospect, accepts, then you're halfway to getting the order.

balance sheet closing strategy: A major closing strategy in which you add what it costs the customer not to have the advantages and benefits of your unique selling points to the competitor's cost to use the products/services. These cost-in-use

Glossary of Terms

figures are then added to the price to get the product/service to determine the true bottom line value.

benefits: What the customer gets from your features to fill Business and Human Needs.

bottom-line: The total of the price of the product or service plus what it costs to use it (also called the "total cost of ownership").

business needs: All businesses have four foundational needs: 1) increase profitable revenue, lower costs, enhance their image, and reduce risks. Your Features provide Benefits to meet these needs to motivate purchase. Advantages meet Functional needs and which answers the questions, what it does, and why it's better.

buyer beliefs: Before you or your customer will buy a product or service the decision makers must hold certain beliefs. They must believe that:
    11. A need exists.
    12. They have or share the responsibility to fill the need.
    13. They have or share the authority to fill the need.
    14. The unfulfilled need is causing some discomfort.
    15. The need has priority over other needs.
    16. Your type of solution will fill the need.
    17. You, your company and product/service have the capability and credibility to fill the need.
    18. Your solution to the exclusion of competing solutions is the best solution.
    19. The price for the solution is less than the value to be received.
    20. Your plan for implementation will be successful.

If a buyer belief is missing or weak, then a specifically related objection will occur - spoken or not.

buyer roles: Within a sale, different decision makers make different types of decisions about different aspects of the sale.

Strategic Sales Plan

The final authority makes decisions concerning return on investment. The specifier makes decisions regarding performance characteristics and cost justification. The negotiator makes decisions about the number of features versus the amount of money to be paid. The end user makes decisions about how easy it is to use the product/service. The coach makes decisions about your capability and credibility. The Recommender makes decisions related to how helping you will provide him/her with better service and how it might strengthen certain relationships. Capabilities and credibility are important. One person can play more than one role, and more than one person can play a single role.

buying cycle: The time periods used by companies for routine purchases, monthly, quarterly, annually, etc. This means that if a company buys what you sell annually and they just made the purchase then, even if they want to buy from you after only three months (sales cycle) of interaction, they cannot go ahead until the end of the current contract.

clarifying questions: These are follow up questions used to change the information the prospect might give you from vague generalizations to specific, measurable useful information.

closed-ended questions: Questions that result in a one or two-word response. Generally used when factual information is required. Examples: "Are you the purchasing manager?" "How many widgets do you buy each year?" Words that can initiate closed-ended questions include: is, will, does, which, who, are, when, can.

common ground: The process is to discover what you and the other person share in common. It is usually done with small talk and revolves around safe topics such as the weather, traffic, travel, etc. As more and more items are found to be shared in common, each person sees the other to be more like them. The more they are like them; the more they think they can predict the person's behavior at certain events. After all, they're much like

Glossary of Terms

me; they would probably respond as I would. As such, the ability to extend trust to the other person grows.

communicating your understanding: A method used to establish trust and rapport in which you provide the prospect feedback that shows you truly understand his/her situation. The more the prospect feels that you know what he/she is facing and the constraints and capabilities that impact the solution, the more he/she will trust that your recommendations for a solution will be on target.

competitive comparison closing strategy: A major closing strategy in which you list your Unique Selling Points Features, Advantages and Benefits in a sentence format down the left-hand side of the page. Across the top of the page, you list the names of your competitors, as well as, your company name. Beneath your company's name, you state "Yes" you can provide the Feature, Advantage, and Benefit to each corresponding one listed. Under your competitors, you would state "No" because, being unique to you, this Feature, Advantage, and Benefit would not be available. This is usually laid out in a graph format. Some companies will choose to give the competitors a few yes's now and then to build credibility. You've seen this used with a credit card or software comparisons, and with a company's own products.

corporate value systems: Values are a natural desire for something. In a corporation, they reflect not only needs but also style. For example, all companies need cost containment. One company may buy only the cheapest product/service to meet this need while another may pay more for higher quality because it will last longer. Both companies meet the need, but their value system determines how they will go about doing it. The closer your company's values match those of the prospective customer's values, the easier it will be to do business with them.

cost-to-use: The costs associated with using a product/service such as buying gas for a car, maintenance expenses, insurance

Strategic Sales Plan

premiums and so on must be added in and compared with competing products/services to determine the true long-term value.

credentials: This method of building trust and rapport is designed to establish your personal, your company's and your product's/service's capability and credibility. Stating credentials to a prospect helps them to estimate how much weight to give your recommended solutions. Credentials also become very important during a negotiation.

Customer Value Proposition (CVP): The Customer Value Proposition (CVP) follows a specific format to demonstrate how your company, product, and service will meet the prospect's requirements (that now include your Unique Selling Points - USPs).

Additionally, there are several psychological principles involved to help break any irrational customer loyalty bond, create a balanced thinking strategy on costs and pricing, keep the pressure of time and sense of urgency on the prospective customer's shoulders, and accommodate both ends of the personality based decision-making continuum.

- Situational Analysis: Present your understanding of the situation.
- Value (Economic and Other Impact): Quantify the seriousness of the problem using their facts and figures.
- Selection Criteria: List the specifications in the left-hand column (one item per row) and how you will meet them in the right-hand column. Use irrefutable logic to confirm how your company can meet the criteria. If needed, put the multi-bid summary form in this space by listing the options in the Your Capabilities column or attach the form at the end.
- Investment and Financial Comparison Analysis: This can be presented in a "balance sheet" style format to show the comparison between current costs and future

Glossary of Terms

costs or you can use a straight listing of prices. Here is where you could include the financial equivalency section to get to compare apples to apples. The "triple-bid" or "multi-bid" summary format can also be used or referenced here and provided as supporting material.
- Plan for Implementation: The steps to move the project forward and close the sale. Note that within the first 5 to 7 steps one item must be completed, another item to complete without the need for the customer to make a decision and a third step that provides some form of feedback to the customer.

decision makers: See buyer roles.

decision making influences: See buyer roles.

educational questions: These are two-part questions. The first part is used to orient and educate about a specific topic. The second part is used to determine specific information about the topic as it has now been framed. For example, "The containers are made of plastic so they won't rust, how will that help you reduce your container replacement budget?" (See FAB-TEA Value Selling Model).

FAB-TEA Value Selling Model: Feature, Advantage, Benefit – Tell, Explain, Ask. Tell the Feature, Explain it with the Advantage, and Ask about the Benefit. For example, "The containers are made of (F) plastic so they (A) won't rust, how will that help you (B) reduce your container replacement budget?"

face-saving: Prevent a person from embarrassment or shame. This could include handling a customer's objection in a way that shows them support their current understanding and belief before you provide them with new information that would move them to make a different decision. For example, if the prospect says that your price is too high, and you respond with, "no you're wrong," and go on to demonstrate just how wrong the prospect

81

Strategic Sales Plan

is, then you may win the battle, but you may not win the sale. Rather, transition sentences are used to help the prospect save face by first supporting (not agreeing) with their belief, then providing information that would help them draw a different conclusion. "That's a good point, and I'm glad you brought it up because that was the same conclusion I drew when I first looked at this. Then I found out..."

features: Characteristics of your products, services, company, and self, that do something (advantage) to solve or prevent problems.

human needs: All humans have these four fundamental needs: 1) Money needs, 2) Safety needs, 3) Esteem needs, & 4) Pleasure needs. They can be combined create other needs. For example, combining safety with esteem can create power needs. And by extending the definitions and scope, they can individually include other needs. For example, the pleasure need also includes the need for order, symmetry, closure, happiness, and beauty.

interim action plan: A written plan developed at the end of a sales call that lists action items both the seller and the prospect agree to do between now and the next meeting. The action items are those that are necessary to continue to advance the sale according to the overall strategic sales plan. The time and date for the next meeting, location, and participants are also identified at the bottom of the plan. When this format is used, it will meet the requirements for most ISO 9000 type programs.

irrefutable logic: Features, Advantages, and Benefits that are logically connected so that if the Feature is purchased, the Benefits will follow. For example, if your service is available 24 hours, 7 days a week, then the customer would have the ability to have services performed in a timelier manner, should they need them after the regular business hours (8-5, five days a week) than your competitor offers.

Glossary of Terms

knock out questions: Questions that would immediately disqualify a prospect. For example, to buy certain drugs at the pharmacy, you must be a licensed physician. An answer of "no" to the question, "Are you a licensed physician?" would immediately determine this person to be ineligible to purchase. Similarly, many companies have minimum order sizes, shipping or pick up requirements, and other conditions that would disqualify a buyer. During prospecting, these questions are usually asked very early in the qualifying process to save prospecting time for those who can qualify to buy.

logistical buying process: Companies have different procedures in how they buy. One company may only require one person to sign the requisition, while another may require several different people to sign. Some companies may process the paperwork as it comes in, while others may only do it once a month. The route the paperwork and product and service delivery takes could vary from one company to the next.

market: A group of individuals who share some common characteristics. See market segment.

market segment: A more narrowly defined subset of a larger market. For example, manufacturing is a market and electronics manufacturing is a segment. Utilities is a market and telephone services, electric power, gas generation, etc., are segments.

milestones: A milestone is a goal that is achieved when the steps or action items it represents are completed.

next step closing strategy: Stating the "next step" in the strategic sales plan that will need to be accomplished or asking the prospect what they see as the next step is part of a closing strategy that concludes the steps accomplished to date and advances the sale to the next step.

objection preventing, preempting, and responding strategies notebook: A notebook that contains prevention, preemption, and response strategies to known objections related to what you sell. Most objections are common and known to the seller. The Sales Professional uses the notebook to prepare for calls in which specific objections are anticipated. One way in which objections can be anticipated is by identifying areas where the competitor is strong. Objections occur when one or more of the "buyer beliefs" are missing or weak and are triggered when a salesperson starts to present.

open-ended questions: Compel the respondent to provide more than a one or two-word response. Words that can initiate open-ended questions include, tell me, explain, describe, compare, how, elaborate, what, why.

orienting questions: These are used to focus the topics of conversation where you're strong, the competitor is weak, and the customer has needs.

ownership question closing strategy: A question posed to the prospect in which the only way he/she can answer it is by seeing themselves owning your product or service. For example, asking the prospect where he/she would put your product in their building would mean that the prospect would have to visualize the product in a certain place. The underlying assumption is that the prospect would not see having your product in a certain place unless he/she owned it.

pacing and leading: A "Neuro-linguistic programming" method of establishing trust and rapport. The theory is that the more someone is like us, the more we will extend trust. Pacing is the process of getting in step with the prospect by mirroring and matching them in behavior, posture, manner, speech, dress, and so on. It includes communicating to the prospect that you understand where they are "in thought." For example, in a retail sales situation, you observe a prospective customer looking for a coat. To pace the customer, you would render a comment such as, "I see you're looking at the S&S brand coat." To this, it is very difficult to deny or say "No thanks, just looking." Leading

Glossary of Terms

is the process in which rapport (harmony) has been established, and now you take the lead, and the customer paces you. This automatically happens when you care about the person and have a mutual goal to work towards together. See also psychologically connected.

plan of action closing strategy: This major closing strategy can be used throughout the sales process in which a plan is developed to move through one or more steps in the strategic sales plan. The plan of action can be developed with the customer, as you would do with the interim action plan or can be presented to the customer as you would with the plan for implementation close.

plan for implementation closing strategy: This major closing strategy is designed to use input gained from the customer about their specific logistical buying process, need fulfillment priority, timing issues and the action items that need to be completed to wrap up the sale and delivery.

price to get: This is the price of the product or service. It is the "top-line" in the formula to get to the "bottom-line." The top-line does not include operational costs associated with using it.

principled negotiations: Negotiation procedure based on following certain principles rather than adversarial tricks. For example, one principle is to use "standards of legitimacy" to set prices and costs rather than wants and needs. For example, using industry standards or some other mutually agreed upon benchmark removes trust and pressure from the negotiation.

profile: A template of characteristics a group of customers has in common.

psychologically connected: A state of mind in which you are in close and in deep harmony with another person that all distractions such as sound, temperature, and disruptive thoughts do not intrude on the communication.

Strategic Sales Plan

psychological truth: A process used to gain the right to be heard. "If you sincerely try to understand another person's point of view first then, they become psychologically obligated to try to understand yours." Psychological truth is achieved through the use of "active listening skills" and is demonstrated in the Situational Analysis step in the Customer Value Proposition.

question types: Different question structures that elicit different responses. Examples:
- open-ended questions are used to elicit information about the topic of the question
- closed ended questions to elicit a one or two-word response
- educational questions are two-part questions used to orient and educate about a specific topic, then to ask a question about a specific part of the information given
- rhetorical questions are used when the desired answer is known or obvious (isn't it, don't you agree?)
- clarifying questions are used as follow up questions to elicit specific data
- ownership questions are used to cause the buyer to see him/herself already owning what you sell to answer the question
- alternative choice questions are designed to give the prospect a choice between two or more alternatives where any selected answer always signifies that he/she is going ahead

rhetorical questions: This is a question the answer to which you already know or is one that you want to elicit. They are commonly used to get an agreement, establish a positive response set and get an agreement that the other person understands you. Common structures for rhetorical questions include: isn't it, can't you, doesn't it, wouldn't you, wasn't it, haven't they, don't we, shouldn't it, couldn't it, don't you agree, won't you, right. These structures can be used at the beginning, in the middle or at the end of the question. This questioning

Glossary of Terms

strategy can be done non-verbally by simply making a statement then moving your head up and down to signify yes.

right to speak: Prospects and customers alike are not willing or ready to hear your ideas for solutions until they are assured that you fully understand their situation. You gain the right to speak and be heard by actively listening to them. Active listening skills such as using acceptance responses, repeating, paraphrasing and summarizing to make sure you heard correctly, and asking clarifying questions when you are unclear, all communications to the person that you heard and understand. When you summarize and feedback all that you now know about the person's situation, and they accept your understanding as accurate, then you have earned the right to speak, be heard and have your recommendations taken seriously. (See also psychological truth and situational analysis.)

sales cycle: How long it usually takes to obtain an account of a certain size and in a specific market segment. See also buying cycle.

situational analysis: The process of seeking targeted information in a specified area, then providing feedback to the prospect or customer regarding critical information that you learned from them. When the prospect or customer confirms that you have read the situation correctly, then based on your credentials, you have earned the right to speak, be heard and have your recommendations taken seriously.

skepticism: A form of objection elicited when the salesperson makes claims that are hard to believe. This causes the prospect to require proof of performance. This objection is common to sales models in which a problem is discovered, and then the salesperson presents his/her solution without first structuring and factoring in "irrefutable logic." Through the use of irrefutable logic, the salesperson would ask the prospect to make the claims rather than the salesperson (See irrefutable logic and the FAB-TEA Value Selling Model).

state dependent learning: We recall information better in the same situation in which we learned it. For example, if you study in a relaxed environment with a gentle rain falling, then you will recall that information when tested in a relaxed environment with a gentle rain falling. In prospecting, by being in front of the prospect through the mail, advertisements, newsletters, phone conversations, in-person visits, referrals and so on, under different environmental and mental conditions over time, then the impact of each contact is leveraged by the previous contacts experienced under different conditions. Making contact under the conditions in which the prospect would normally need your product or service would increase the probability that they would think of you the next time they needed your type of product or service.

statements of interest: In principled negotiating it is preferred to present what you are interested in accomplishing rather than specific demands (statements of position). For example, stating that you are interested in obtaining a "fair wage" leaves you open to using "acceptable industry standards." However, making a statement of position such as, "I won't take less than $25.00 an hour," leaves you open to pressure and embarrassment if you wind up backing down to $20.00 per hour.

statements of position: See statements of interest.

strategic sales plan: A listing of all the steps that must be accomplished by both the seller and the buyer for a sale to complete. The plan is adjusted based on the size and complexity of the sale. This plan can be written, i.e., a listing of the common 44 steps in the sales process or known through experience.

strategy: The art and skill of looking at the big picture surrounding an endeavor, defining the major components and their relative movement to accomplish objectives. In general, the strategy is defined as "what" must be done whereas tactics are defined as "how" to do it. (See also tactic.)

Glossary of Terms

subjective costs: Soft costs usually of an emotional or belief-oriented nature. Peace of mind, feelings of security, frustrations, hassle, stress, confidence, esteem and so on make up the subjective costs that influence buying decisions.

tactic: A specific method, step or action item employed to cause movement of a part of a strategy. In general, the strategy is defined as the game plan and tactics are defined as the steps or action items to implement steps in the plan.

time management organization system: A system that helps organize activities within available time resources according to some priority setting standards. Usually includes an appointment calendar with accompanying dated "to do list" for action items that can be done during discretionary time.

transition sentences: The transition sentence is a diplomatic way to different or opposing information. With transition sentences you can:

- Support without agreeing.
- Help them save face.
- Prevent arguments.
- Pull rather than push (Judo strategy).
- Prepare them to receive new information.

For example:

"I understand how you feel because that's how I felt when I first came across this, and then I found out . . ."
"That makes sense, and it also makes sense when you add . . ."
"Under ordinary circumstances that would apply, however, when we . . ."
"That's what I said when I first heard about this; then I found out . . ."
"And that's exactly why I'm calling..."

STRATEGIC SALES PLAN

"That's true, and when we compare the two on their abilities to ____, ____, and ____ (USPs), it makes sense to explore the possibility that there's more to this than meets the eye, doesn't it?

value selling: a particular type of sales process in which the selling is usually done during a strategically designed interview rather than during the presentation. All value selling models will help prevent or minimize price pressure. The Value Selling Strategies P.R.O.S.P.E.C.T. Model, ACE Value Selling Model, and FAB-TEA Value Selling are examples of value selling models taught be Sales Training International.

Value Selling Strategies P.R.O.S.P.E.C.T. Model: Called the $E=MC^2$ of value selling models because it's timeless and effective.

Profile and qualify

Research prospect and competitor

Orient the prospect in areas the competitor analysis shows you're strong, the competitor is weak and, your research shows the prospect has needs.

Symptoms are the missing Advantages and Benefits of your Unique Selling Point's (USPs) Feature.

Problem is the prospect doesn't have the USP's Feature.

Effects and consequences of the problem financially, emotionally, subjectively in the past, present, and future.

Criteria are set to get the USPs that will do away with the pain and the associated costs (missing Advantages and Benefits) by solving the problem (missing Feature). You do this by getting the USP Feature. Circular, but irrefutably logical.

Glossary of Terms

Triggering Events are the logistics steps of advancing the sale.

ACE Value Selling Model

Anxieties about the missing Advantages and Benefits
Costs of not having the Advantages and Benefits
Expectations of getting the Feature that provides the Advantages and Benefits.

FAB TEA Value Selling Model

Tell the Feature
Explain the **A**dvantage
Ask about the **B**enefits

value selling process example:

For this example, we'll use the plastic containers.

Feature: Plastic containers
Advantage: Won't rust
Benefit: Eliminate budget for container replacement due to rust, rust stain cleaning, and returned damaged products in the rusted container.

The Seller discovered during the Profile and Research phases that this prospect has to replace a lot of steel containers each month due to rust.

By the numbers in this Strategic Sales Plan.

Step 18 – Focus the topics of conversation on your Unique Selling points.
   Seller: "In thinking about the materials your containers are made of there, are three areas that can jump out at me: First is the rust stains and how that looks to

91

Strategic Sales Plan

prospective customers on a plant tour, second is the amount of damaged product from the rust, and the third is the rusty container replacement budget. Which of these would you like to focus on first?

Buyer selects budget.

Step 19 – Identify the signs caused by your Unique Selling Points missing Advantages and Benefits.
Seller: ". . . What are your greatest concerns about the size of your replacement budget? Tell me what's going on there.

Buyer explains that with increased sales come increased numbers of containers that rust and have to be replaced.

Step 20 – Confirm the problems caused by the missing USPs
Seller: "That a problem with using steel in this coastal climate. It's going to rust."

Without pausing continue to Step 21.

Step 21 – Quantify their costs of not having your USPs to establish the value of the solution.
Seller: "How many barrels are you replacing each month? In addition to buying the containers, what other costs are involved with that?

Buyer explains that staff has to transfer the product from the rusting container to a new one. It's a nasty job that no one wants to do. Sometimes they subcontract that job out, but that just adds to the cost. Also, they have to scrub the rust stains off the storage facilities; again, more cost.

Seller and buyer agree to get the specific numbers involved in these costs from the buyer's records and confirm them at their next meeting.

Glossary of Terms

Step 22 – Set your USPs as specifications that must be met to solve the problems.

> Seller: "So one of your requirements to consider another supplier is that they could provide you with containers made of a material that won't rust and be just as strong as the ones you're using now. Is that pretty much where we are now?"
>
> Buyer agrees.

Step 23 – Competitor proof with Benefits Questions.

> Seller: "In addition to what we've talked about, what other benefits do you see getting with using containers that won't rust? What about the staff who are out there scrubbing the stains and changing the product? How would the sales and marketing people like this? Who else would benefit from going to the non-rusting containers?"

Step 24 – Complete the interviews with key decision makers.
Step 25 – Validate any cost-benefit data that used industry standards.

At this time, the seller is continuing to complete the process with the current decision maker, so this step doesn't come into play yet.

Complete Logistics Steps

Step 26 – Advise and get agreement on the net steps to advance the sale.

> Seller: "Between now and when we get back together next week if you could confirm what those costs are in real dollars, please. We'll want to clearly demonstrate that using non-rusting containers will dramatically improve the budget outlook over the time it will take to transition. Who else would you want at our next meeting to take a look at a couple of containers of this size?"

Strategic Sales Plan

Step 27 – Outline feedback loops, milestones, measurements, and follow up process.

> Seller: "A major milestone will be when we complete the proof of concept. Another will be when new production goes exclusively to non-rusting containers, and another will be when all the steel containers are gone. What other milestones do you see we should measure?"

Step 28 – Develop product/service delivery phase-in plans.

Step 29 – Determine product/service availability.

> Seller: "Given that the costs for making the change will result in a lower bottom-line and after we complete the proof of concept, how many containers would you put in your initial order, I want to make sure our inventory is available."

Most of the Strategic Sales Plan steps can be done over the phone in a matter of minutes. And in other larger or more complex sales, it could take months.

unique selling points (USPs): Features, advantages, and benefits you, your company and the products/services you offer that your competitors do not offer. Used to differentiate what you sell and how you sell it from the competition.

Differentiating Factors

The following list is intended to help stimulate thinking and brainstorming to identify some of the less obvious factors that can be used to differentiate your company, product/service, and self from the competition. Ask how you are different than the competition in each of these areas. For each area where you are different, ask what it costs the customer not to have your method of doing things.

COMPANY
organizational infrastructure, plans, emphasis, i.e., quality, team, planning, financial stability, communications, corporate integrity, inter-departmental knowledge, reputation, experience in the industry, track records, i.e., safety, environmental.

PERSONNEL
training, commitment, capabilities, special skills/departments, experience in the industry, quality of professional, turn over that impacts relationships.

FACILITIES
location, number, redundancies/backup, modernization, capabilities, accessibility, flexibility.

MATERIALS
feedstock quality, source/availability, procurement processes, uniform product.

MANUFACTURING
product line - breadth/depth, product superiority, reliability engineering, lead time requirements, special or proprietary manufacturing processes, product consistency, quality assurance/controls, safety and environmental record, custom capabilities, flexibility, real-time order status monitoring,

outsourcing, short notice changes, special size orders capabilities.

DISTRIBUTION
distribution system, packaging, shipping/transporting, tracking/monitoring, inventory - special arrangements, disposal/EPA standards.

RESEARCH & DEVELOPMENT
capabilities, focus, i.e., customer, market, product, number of test runs to ensure consistency, R&D technical support.

CUSTOMER SUPPORT SERVICES
order center, on call 24 hours a day, customer service follow-up calls, marketing research for customer support, training, knowledgeable staff, technical support services, quick resolution of problems, documentation, warranties, guarantees, simplified paperwork, easy ordering process, customer interaction analysis.

SALES
customer to rep ratio, customer relationships, team approach, knowledge of customer's business, corporate account manager, "partnering" relationships, national account manager, diagnostic and value-based approach to selling, specialists, technical competence, responsive to customer needs

Strategic Sales Plan
Sales Process Steps for B2B Selling

Profile and Qualify Sales Prospect

1. Compare the prospect with the profile of your most desirable customers.
2. Identify the decision-makers.
3. Identify the initial people to contact.
4. Select and sequence methods of contact.
5. Set your call objectives.
6. Make contact.
7. Establish trust and rapport.
8. Qualify the prospect for the current sales opportunity.
   GO / NO GO

Research the Prospect's Needs

9. Research prospect's products, services, and company.
10. Research prospect's critical processes.
11. Research prospect's business plans.
12. Identify the potential for your other products and services.

Conduct the Competitor Analyses

13. Identify your external and internal competitors.
14. Conduct the competitor analyses.
15. Update your list of Unique Selling Points.
16. Identify potential objections.
    GO / NO GO

Establish the Value of What You Sell

17. Prevent, preempt, and respond to potential objections.
18. Focus the topics of conversation on your Unique Selling Points (USPs).

STRATEGIC SALES PLAN

19. Identify the signs caused by your USPs missing Advantages and Benefits.
20. Confirm the problems caused by the missing USPs.
21. Quantify their costs of not having your USPs to establish the value of the solution.
22. Set your USPs as specifications that must be met to solve the problems.
23. Competitor Proof with Benefits Questions.
24. Complete the interviews with key decision-makers.
    GO / NO GO
25. Validate of any cost-benefit data that used industry standards.

Complete the Logistics Steps

26. Advise and get agreement on the next steps to advance the sale.
27. Outline feedback loops, milestones, measurements, and follow up process.
28. Develop product/service delivery phase-in plans.
29. Determine product/service.
    GO / NO GO
30. Complete required pre-purchase approvals.
    GO / NO GO
31. Exchange any additional data, specifications, or financial information.
32. Identify and prepare your Recommenders to be your Champions.

Propose, Present, and Negotiate

33. Prepare and submit the Customer Value Proposition (CVP).
34. Conduct the sales presentation using the CVP format.
35. Prospect affirms your ability to meet criteria.
    GO / NO GO
36. Conclude final negotiations.
37. Final budget approval received.
    GO / NO GO

38. Contract signed, or letter of engagement received
39. Customer notifies current supplier(s).

Deliver Your Product & Services

40. Identify and arrange to meet the critical support people.
41. Identify specific End Users involved in the project.
42. Conduct quality checks of the product and service delivery.

Manage Your Account

43. Implement sales activities to competitor proof and grow the account.
44. Recognize the signs that your account may be in trouble before it's too late.

About the Author

Dr. Robert "Bob" DeGroot, M.Ed., D.C.H. is the founder and president of Sales Training International. He is a bestselling author, counselor, consultant, sales professional, and trainer with over 30 years of experience in the fields of sales, training, and psychology.

After completing his military service in the US Coast Guard, he attended college where he earned a Bachelor's in Psychology and a Master of Education in School Psychology from Texas State University. Later in life, he earned a Doctorate in Clinical Hypnotherapy from the American Institute of Hypnotherapy. He's had rewarding careers in both the mental health sciences, education, and in sales.

The magic in sales happened for Bob when he discovered the psychology that made sales techniques work successfully in some situations but not in others. His studies in human motivation, buying behavior, and persuasion led him to develop a different perspective that is evident in this latest book.

Starting with his first book, "Psychology for Successful Selling" published in 1988, Bob has written over 70 training courses, 50 Web-based training courses, several paperbacks, and dozens of eBooks in the professions of sales, sales management, and customer service.

www.SalesHelp.com

Other books by Robert DeGroot

Available from booksellers everywhere.

Sales Titles

1. Objection Free Selling: How to Prevent, Preempt, and Respond to Every Sales Objection You Get (Best Seller)
2. Value Selling Strategies P.R.O.S.P.E.C.T. Model (Best Seller)
3. Features - Advantages – Benefits (Best Seller)
4. Telephone Cold Call with Voicemail Strategy (Best Seller)
5. Sales Prospecting: The Hunt for New Business
6. Goal Setting for Success
7. Research Prospect & Competitor
8. Competitor Analysis
9. Trust & Rapport Building
10. Profile and Qualify Sales Prospect
11. Key Decision Maker Roles
12. Passive Letter Contact Series
13. Interest mailer Contact Series
14. Keep in Touch Contact Series
15. Networking Contact Strategy
16. Asking for Referrals
17. Teleblitz
18. Funnel Management
19. Ratio Management
20. Time & Territory Management
21. Block the Competition
22. Benefit Questions Create Attitudes

STRATEGIC SALES PLAN

Sales Management Titles

1. Reseller Strategy (Best Seller)
2. Career Path for Sales Professionals
3. Interviewing and Hiring Sales Professionals
4. Sales Professionals Performance Appraisal
5. Sales Coach
6. Peer-to-Peer Sales Coaching
7. Creating and Leading a Motivating Sales Culture
8. Effective Meeting Planning and Facilitating

Customer Service Titles

1. Telephone Etiquette for Business (Best Seller)
2. Active Listening Skills for Business (Best Seller)
3. Defusing Customer Anger
4. Problem Solving Model for Business
5. Managing Customer Expectations
6. Email Etiquette for Business
7. Stress Control at Work

www.ingramcontent.com/pod-product-compliance
Lightning Source LLC
Chambersburg PA
CBHW050602300426
44112CB00013B/2027